# I Had

# a

# Pet Frog

*100 pets and animals that will make you smile,
chuckle and laugh out loud*

# I Had a Pet Frog

*100 pets and animals that will make you smile, chuckle and laugh out loud*

## By Wan-Yu Chao & Ronald Kerble

## Illustrations by Christine Liao

**I Had a Pet Frog Co.**

Library of Congress Control Number: 2010927221

ISBN: 978-0-9827133-0-3

Cover design by Dr. Wan-Yu Chao & Ronald Kerble
Cover illustration by Christine Liao

**Attention: Schools, Businesses and Clubs:**

This book is available at a quantity discount with bulk purchases for educational, business, fundraising or sales promotional use. For Information, please email to the publisher at
**customerservice@ihadapetfrog.com**

*From our family to your family*
*with our love of animals and*
*a sense of humor*


從我們的家庭到您的家庭
謹獻上我們對動物之愛和幽默感

I had a pet frog

Who liked to smoke.

I told him it was an unhealthy habit,

Then he croaked.

I had a pet duck

Who saw a famous doctor.

I asked him what he thought,

Then he said, "He was a quack."

I had a pet hyena

Who was always getting into trouble.

I told him he'll get punished,

Then he laughed.

I had a pet cow

Who only ate French fries.

I told her to eat healthy,

Then she went sour.

I had a pet bear

Who liked to chase hunters.

I told him it was dangerous,

Then he got stuffed.

I had a pet rock

Who was a detective.

I asked why he was so good,

Then he said, "I leave no stone unturned."

I had a pet snake

Who liked to play baseball.

I told him he could not bat,

Then he missssssssssssed.

I had a pet toad

Who was a great jumper.

I told him to look before he leaped,

Then he hit a tad pole.

I had a pet giraffe

Who didn't like playing pirates with his friends.

I asked him why,

Then he said he was always the lookout.

I had a pet horse

Who liked to travel.

I told him the flights were full,

Then he hoofed it.

I had a pet praying mantis

Who sat and prayed.

I asked what he was praying for,

Then he said, "Lunch!"

I had a pet bird

Who got up late.

I asked why not early,

Then he said, "I hate worms."

I had a pet cat

Who always used a computer.

I asked why she liked it so much,

Then she said, "I like the mouse."

I had a pet turtle

Who served in the war.

I asked how he was,

Then he said, "Shell shocked."

I had a pet octopus

Who wrote with a pen in each arm.

I told him I didn't like his writings,

Then he inked.

I had a pet deer

Who was looking for a mate and a job.

I told her don't get your hopes up,

Then she found a buck.

———

I had a pet goose

Who loved driving my car.

I told her you need a license,

Then she honked.

I had a pet eel

Who wasn't a very good student.

I told him he got an A,

Then he was shocked.

I had a pet
chameleon

Who was so very
stubborn.

I told him to
grow up,

Then he wouldn't
change.

I had a pet parrot

Who was captured by the enemy.

I told him to keep quiet,

Then he talked.

———

I had a pet kangaroo

Who was very slow.

I told him to get going,

Then he hopped to it.

I had a pet mosquito

Who liked the bright lights.

I told him to stay away,

Then he got buzzed.

I had a pet snake

Who had a blind date.

I asked if she was nice,

Then he said, "She had a hissy fit."

———

I had a pet donkey

Who loved comedy clubs.

I told him he shouldn't go,

Then he laughed his ass off.

I had a pet cow

Who had a date.

I asked if he was nice,

Then she said like no utter.

I had a pet porcupine

Who went out to lunch
with friends.

I told him to bring
cash,

Then he got stuck with
the bill.

I had a pet porcupine

Who went out to lunch with friends.

I told him to bring extra cash this time,

Then he stuck them with the bill.

———

I had a pet rabbit

Who loved to dance.

I said go to the disco,

Then he did the bunny hop.

I had a pet rhino

Who never did what he was told.

I sent him to bed without supper,

Then he got the point.

I had a pet owl

Who was not very brave.

I told him to be careful,

Then he screeched.

———

I had a pet pig

Who worked three jobs.

I told him to relax,

Then he brought home the bacon.

I had a pet Dalmatian

Who loved shopping.

I told her to stay in line,

Then she lost her spot.

I had a pet boa
constrictor

Who was very
affectionate.

I told her not
to hug,

Then she
squeezed.

I had a pet spider

Who had a date.

I asked why he was so nervous,

Then he said, "She's a Black Widow."

———

I had a pet goat

Who liked to drink beer.

I asked him where he was going,

Then he said, "The baaaar, the baaaar."

I had a pet elephant

Who loved to travel.

I told him to pack light,

Then he packed one trunk.

I had a pet lobster

Who was very very shy.

I told him his fly was down,

Then he turned red.

I had a pet alligator

Who was going away.

I said see you later gator,

Then he said, "In a while, crocodile."

I had a pet pony

Who went to the mall.

I asked what he was looking for,

Then he said, "Horse shoes."

———

I had a pet owl

Who was very smart in school.

I told him there was only one A,

Then he asked, "Whoo…Whoo?"

I had a pet cow

Who loved the theater.

I asked where he was going,

Then he said, "The mooooovies."

I had a pet
jellyfish

Who was bothered by
bullies.

I told him to stand up
to them,

Then he said,

"I have no backbone."

I had a pet leopard

Who ran away from home.

I looked and looked,

Then he was spotted.

———

I had a pet zebra

Who joined the military.

I asked about promotions,

Then he said, "I have to earn my stripes."

I had a pet lion

Who played professional sports.

I asked him why he did it,

Then he said, "The roar of the crowd."

I had a pet
gorilla

Who was very very
hungry.

I told him the restaurants were
full,

Then he went ape.

I had a pet fire ant

Who did aerobics.

I asked him why,

Then he said he liked the burn.

———

I had a pet mammoth

Who was going away.

I asked him where,

Then he said, "Tuskegee."

I had a pet dog

Who was a great actor.

I asked him to show me something,

Then he played dead.

I had a pet spider

Who loved computers.

I told her to go on line,

Then she surfed the web.

I had a pet sheep

Who was very political.

I asked how her party did,

Then she said, "Baaaaaaaad!"

I had a pet caterpillar

Who was into real estate.

I asked how he started,

Then he said, "I rented my cocoon."

———

I had a pet octopus

Who went on a date.

I asked how he was,

Then she said, "He was all arms."

I had a pet squid

Who repaired copiers.

I asked him what I should do,

Then he changed my ink.

I had a pet iguana

Who was looking for
a career.

I asked what he wanted to be
when he grew up.

Then he said,
"A bachelor raptor."

I had a pet snail

Who was running for Mayor.

I asked how the campaign was going,

Then he said, "Way too slow."

I had a pet snake

Who was stopped by the police.

I asked if he had a gun,

Then he said, "I was unarmed."

I had a pet cat

Who had a modeling
job.

I asked how she was
doing,

Then she said,

"I'm scratching out a living."

*I had a pet bee*

*Who was bothered by a mosquito.*

*I asked what did you say?*

*Then he said, "Buzz off !"*

*I had a pet canary*

*Who was captured by the enemy.*

*I told him to keep quiet,*

*Then he sang.*

I had a pet pig

Who went out on a date.

I asked how it went,

Then she said he was a bore.

———

I had a pet cow

Who had a date.

I asked her how it went,

Then she said, "He threw the bull."

I had a pet chimpanzee

Who got all A's.

I asked how he did it,

Then he said, "I didn't monkey around."

I had a pet dragon

Who was looking for
a job.

I heard he got
one,

Then he said,

"A knight watchman."

I had a pet gerbil

Who went on a date.

I asked if he was nice,

Then she said, "He was a rat."

———

I had a pet bear

Who had a date.

I asked who he was,

Then she said, "He was a bi-polar bear."

I had a pet cat

Who loved playing the piano.

I asked for a song,

Then she scratched out a tune.

I had a pet oyster

Who had a lovely pearl.

I asked him whom it was for,

Then he clammed up.

I had a pet penguin

Who hated to ski.

I asked him why,

Then he said he hated the snow.

I had a pet pig

Who saw a robbery.

I asked who did it,

Then he squealed.

I had a pet guppy

Who was afraid of the water.

I told him to be smart,

Then he went to fishing school.

———

I had a pet cow

Who loved to drive my car,

I asked her why,

Then she said, "I like to steer."

I had a pet hen

Who was going to get married.

I asked why she didn't,

Then she said she chickened out.

I had a pet dove

Who always dressed very well.

I told him you look good,

Then he said "Cooooool, cooooool."

———

I had a pet chicken

Who was always picking on the rooster.

I asked her why,

Then she said, "He's hen pecked."

I had a pet pig

Who played the stock market.

I asked for a stock tip,

Then he said, "Pork bellies."

I had a pet lobster

Who went on a date.

I asked if he was nice,

Then she said, "He was crabby."

———

I had a pet caterpillar

Who swam in a race.

I asked which event,

Then he said, "The butterfly."

I had a pet dog

Who owned his own business.

I asked if he was a good boss,

Then he barked out orders.

Bark
Bark
Bark

I had a pet rhino

Who got his driving license.

I told him to drive safe,

Then he tooted his own horn.

———

I had a pet duckling

Who loved the ballet.

I asked her what her favorite was,

Then she said, "Swan Lake."

I had a pet firefly

Who did poorly in school.

I asked him why,

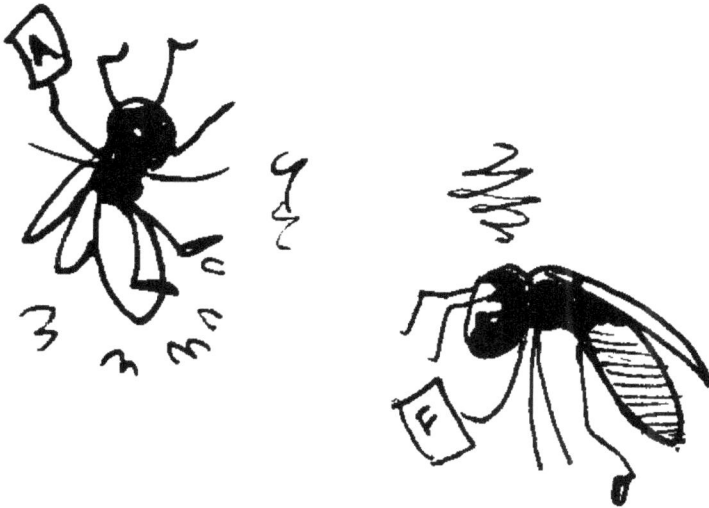

Then he said he's not that bright.

I had a pet Cyclops

Who wanted to be a designer.

I asked why,

Then he said,

"I have an eye for detail."

I had a pet cat

Who dated a rabbit.

I asked how it was going,

Then she coughed up a hare ball.

———

I had a pet rabbit

Who never came when called.

I told him that was not proper,

Then he said, "I don't hare well."

I had a pet parrot

Who loved using the computer.

I asked her why,

Then she said, "I like to talk on line."

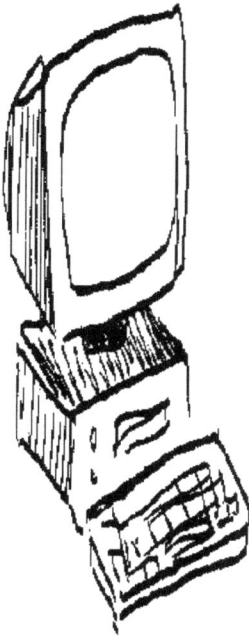

I had a pet tiger

Who went to the doctor.

I asked him what the doctor said,

Then he said, "I need a cat scan."

———

I had a pet pig

Who had a date.

I asked her how it was,

Then she said, "He was a swine."

I had a pet firefly

Who went on a date.

I asked how it was,

Then she said, "He lights up my life."

I had a pet lobster

Who owned his own business.

I asked how he did it,

Then he said,

"I clawed my way to the top."

———

I had a pet cow

Who went to the baseball game.

I asked him where he sat,

Then he said, "The bullpen."

I had a pet bird

Who loved playing golf.

I asked how he did,

Then he said, "I eagled!"

I had a pet tiger

Who lost his job as a
night watchman,

I asked what happened,

Then he said he took a
cat nap.

I had a pet bee

Who had a rash.

I asked what the doctor said,

Then he said, "I have hives."

———

I had a pet dog

Who wanted to be an attorney.

I asked him why,

Then he said to be a legal beagle.

I had a pet bird

Who had a license to
drive.

I asked where she was
going,

Then she said, "South
for the winter."

I had a pet shark

Who went to a home
improvement shop.

I asked what he got,

Then he said,
"A hammer head."

I had a pet frog

Who owned three condos.

I told him I was buying,

Then he leaped at the offer.

———

I had a pet frog

Who had a pet firefly.

I asked why,

Then he said he needed a night light.

I had a pet rabbit

Who was a great leader.

I asked him how,

Then he shouted, "Hop to it!"

# INDEX

## L

Leopard, 40
Lion, 41
Lobster, 34, 72, 82

## M

Mammoth, 44
Mosquito, 21, 56

## O

Octopus, 15, 48
Owl, 28, 36
Oyster, 64

## P

Parrot, 20, 79
Penguin, 65
Pig, 28, 58, 66, 71, 80
Pony, 36
Porcupine, 24, 26
Praying mantis, 11

## R

Rabbit, 26, 78, 91
Rhino, 27, 74
Rock, 6
Rooster, 70

## S

Shark, 88
Sheep, 47
Snail, 52
Snake, 7, 22, 53
Spider, 32, 46
Squid, 49

## T

Tad pole, 8
Tiger, 80, 84
Toad, 8
Turtle, 14

## Z

Zebra, 40

Thank you to our **Chuckle Committee,**
Marc, Joan, Lauren, Maureen and Nancy for
your time, love and great sense of humor.


**See Dr. Wan-Yu Chao
&
Ronald Kerble's
other
publications**


I Had a Pet Frog Coloring Book
*Pets and animals with English and Chinese words*


I Had a Pet Frog Calendars


How to Make a Christmas North Pole Decoration
**The ultimate holiday decoration project for families,
clubs, youth groups, schools & churches**


I Had a Pet Frog T-shirts


@


**www.ihadapetfrog.com**

Now it's your turn to share with us an ingenious joke with your own creative illustration or wonderful photograph.

Using the same format, please send your humorous work to us at

ronaldkerble@ihadapetfrog.com

Please visit us at

**www.ihadapetfrog.com**

## Your creation

I had a pet_____

Who _____

I _____

Then _____


Your illustration or picture here.